TOWARD ARAB-ISRAELI PEACE

TOWARD ARAB-ISRAELI PEACE

REPORT OF A STUDY GROUP

THE BROOKINGS INSTITUTION

Washington, D.C.

Copyright © 1988 by
THE BROOKINGS INSTITUTION
1775 Massachusetts Avenue, N.W., Washington, D.C. 20036
Library of Congress Catalog Card Number: 88-070490
ISBN 0-8157-7291-2
9 8 7 6 5 4 3 2 1

THE BROOKINGS INSTITUTION is an independent organization devoted to nonpartisan research, education, and publication in economics, government, foreign policy, and the social sciences generally. Its principal purposes are to aid in the development of sound public policies and to promote public understanding of issues of national importance.

The Institution was founded on December 8, 1927, to merge the activities of the Institute for Government Research, founded in 1916, the Institute of Economics, founded in 1922, and the Robert Brookings Graduate School of Economics and Government, founded in 1924.

The Board of Trustees is responsible for the general administration of the Institution, while the immediate direction of the policies, program, and staff is vested in the President, assisted by an advisory committee of the officers and staff. The by-laws of the Institution state: "It is the function of the Trustees to make possible the conduct of scientific research, and publication, under the most favorable conditions, and to safeguard the independence of the research staff in the pursuit of their studies and in the publication of the results of such studies. It is not a part of their function to determine, control, or influence the conduct of particular investigations or the conclusions reached."

The President bears final responsibility for the decision to publish a manuscript as a Brookings book. In reaching his judgment on the competence, accuracy, and objectivity of each study, the President is advised by the director of the appropriate research program and weighs the views of a panel of expert outside readers who report to him in confidence on the quality of the work. Publication of a work signifies that it is deemed a competent treatment worthy of public consideration but does not imply endorsement of conclusions or recommendations.

The Institution maintains its position of neutrality on issues of public policy in order to safeguard the intellectual freedom of the staff. Hence interpretations or conclusions in Brookings publications should be understood to be solely those of the authors and should not be attributed to the Institution, to its trustees, officers, or other staff members, or to the organizations that support its research.

Foreword

IN 1975 the Brookings Institution organized a study group of foreign policy specialists with a particular interest in the Middle East. The result was *Toward Peace in the Middle East,* a report that had considerable influence on the Carter administration's policies toward the Arab-Israeli conflict.

Early in 1987 William B. Quandt, a senior fellow in the Foreign Policy Studies program and a participant in the first "Brookings Report," formed a new study group with the objective of taking a fresh look at the Arab-Israeli peace process. Henry Owen, who had organized the first Brookings study group on the Middle East, was generous with encouragement and advice. The group met for the first time in May 1987 and then monthly from September 1987 through February 1988.

Events in the Middle East often seem to have the capacity to catch us by surprise. At the outset of the group's deliberations, there was concern that Americans were simply not interested in the issue of Arab-Israeli peace. It was not high on the administration's foreign policy agenda and there was little public discussion of the issues. By the time the group concluded its work early this year, Israeli-Palestinian clashes were on the front page of every newspaper and new initiatives for peace were being actively considered.

This report is intended to enrich the discussion of how the United States can best promote Arab-Israeli peace negotiations. It does not offer a blueprint. It does suggest how to get the negotiating process under way and puts forward principles that should inform the efforts of any American president.

The group that produced the report was not homogeneous. Indeed, the exercise was meant to ensure that diverse views were included. The report is of particular interest because the group, despite its differences on many basic points, was still able to reach a broad consensus on how the United States should use its influence on behalf of peace in the Middle East.

In the course of the deliberations that led to this report, encouragement, advice, and support were received from many persons. Special thanks are due to those at Brookings who helped with the production of the report: Judy Buckelew and Susanne Lane, who organized the meetings of the group, kept a record of the proceedings, and produced endless drafts; Robert L. Faherty and Caroline Lalire for editorial assistance that transformed the draft into a finished publication; and John S. Armour, David A. Hamod, and John M. Hills for help in organizing support for the project.

Financial assistance for the project came from the following sources: the Foundation for Middle East Peace, the George Gund Foundation, the John D. and Catherine T. MacArthur Foundation, the Mobil Oil Corporation, Mrs. Harley C. Stevens, and Ezra K. Zilkha. Their support is all the more welcome in that they had no way of knowing what the group would agree upon, or indeed if a report would even be produced. They simply believed the effort was worth making and they offered their help. Needless to say, neither they nor the trustees, officers, and staff members of the Brookings Institution bear any responsibility for the views expressed in this report.

BRUCE K. MACLAURY, *President*
March 1988
Washington, D.C.

Contents

Preface

THIS REPORT, *Toward Arab-Israeli Peace: Report of a Study Group,* is the result of many hours of discussion over a period of nearly one year. Like any collective effort, ours required much give-and-take to reach agreement. The common thread within our diverse group was a genuine commitment to the idea of peace between Israel and its Arab neighbors, as well as a conviction that the United States can and should play a constructive role in moving toward that goal.

Although the group was in agreement on most issues, there were differences of opinion. Most can be traced to divergent judgments about how best to achieve a durable peace between Israel and the Palestinians.

Some members favored some form of Jordanian-Palestinian association or a three-way economic and political umbrella linking Israel, West Bank and Gaza Palestinians, and Jordan in some fashion. They felt that an independent Palestinian state in the West Bank and Gaza would inevitably be irredentist and therefore a source of permanent instability and a threat to Israel's survival as a Jewish state. They doubted that a peace treaty or international guarantees could ensure any lasting constraints on an independent state's military capabilities. In addition, they believed that the Palestine Liberation Organization's (PLO) actions and program threatened American interests and the security of our friends in the region. They felt that regardless of the support the PLO may enjoy among Palestinians, efforts to include the PLO in any negotiations would impede the peace process, not promote it. They believed that there must be a fundamental change in the PLO position and, therefore, the U.S. commitment and law regarding dealings and contact with the PLO should not be altered. They also emphasized that, while Palestinian-Israeli relations are of vital concern, the United States should not discount the importance of state-to-state relationships. Along with Palestinians in the West Bank and Gaza, Arab governments must be the primary participants in direct negotiations and in the peace that follows.[1]

Others felt that a Palestinian state, even if limited to only a part of historic Palestine, would essentially meet Palestinian aspirations, would not be a threat to Israel's security, and would contribute to a lasting political settlement of the conflict between the two claimants to the same land. They also felt that any relationship between the Palestinians and Jordan should be one of equality and should be freely negotiated. In addition, they felt that since the PLO is considered by Palestinians to represent them, it must be directly involved in any negotiations relating to the future of the Palestinian people. They believed that the primary venue for negotiations should be an international conference. Any interim agreement should be negotiated in this context, should be integrally linked to a final resolution of the conflict in a comprehensive peace, and should end the military occupation of the West Bank and Gaza Strip. Finally, they believed that existing obstacles in law and policy to U.S. contacts with the PLO should be removed.[2]

A third view was more agnostic on the details of a final peace settlement, arguing that the proper American role was to get a negotiating process under way and to keep it moving toward an outcome whose precise nature could not be predetermined, but which could reasonably be expected to contribute to regional

---

1. Kenneth Wollack considers all the points in this paragraph to be essential. Other members in the group endorsed some of them.

2. Rashid Khalidi and Fouad Moughrabi consider all the points in this paragraph to be essential. Other members in the group endorsed some of them.

stability by meeting the essential needs of all the concerned parties, especially Israel, Jordan, and the Palestinians.

Our members also disagreed about how explicit the link should be between any transitional arrangements and a comprehensive settlement. Some felt that interim arrangements have intrinsic value and should stand on their own, and that insistence on explicit linkage would make agreement unattainable. Others felt that an agreed sense of direction toward an overall settlement would be necessary if transitional arrangements were to be made acceptable to the Palestinians, Syrians, and other Arabs.

These differences of opinion are, of course, not unique to our group. They are at the heart of Arab-Israeli diplomacy, and each has advocates within the United States and within the region. We have not tried to wish these differences away or to paper them over. We have tried to find acceptable compromise formulations. We have also reached substantial agreement on the nature of American interests in the region, on the realities that will govern the next round of diplomacy, on the need for building firm political foundations for any diplomatic effort, on the importance of an international framework for peacemaking, on the need for transitional steps, and on certain principles that should shape a vision of an overall peace agreement between Arabs and Israelis. This consensus, we feel, is a substantial achievement.

The discussion and drafting that produced this report began in the spring of 1987, a year that ended with the worst outbreak of violence in the West Bank and Gaza since Israel's occupation began in 1967. We have devoted conspicuous, though not exclusive, attention to the Israeli-Palestinian dimension of the Arab-Israeli conflict and to the underlying instability in the occupied territories. The urgency of forward movement in a negotiating process that advances Israeli-Palestinian peace is, to us, a clear imperative for a new American administration. Our judgment rests not merely on headlines of late 1987 and early 1988, but also, and more importantly, on the underlying trends and realities in the region that led to these prolonged disturbances and to our recommendations.

A final note is in order. This report represents a broad consensus on the part of the study group. Not all members feel equally comfortable with each of the recommendations, and in endorsing the report they do not necessarily imply that they agree with each and every formulation therein. The members of the group have all participated as individuals.

SUMMARY OF THE REPORT

Summary

THE STUDY GROUP on Arab-Israeli peacemaking was able to reach broad agreement in seven areas.

1. Urgency

Arab-Israeli peacemaking deserves to be high on the agenda of the next administration. A prolonged impasse in the peace process could endanger American national interests. Recent violent clashes between Israelis and Palestinians are vivid reminders of the explosive situation in the region. At the same time, possible openings toward peace have been created. In short, both dangers and opportunities exist.

2. New Realities

A newly elected president will not be able to get his bearings on the Arab-Israeli conflict simply by evoking the formulas of the past. U.N. Security Council Resolutions 242 and 338, the Camp David Accords, and President Ronald Reagan's proposal of September 1, 1982, contain some useful building blocks. But a serious policy cannot be developed simply by stringing these formulations together. New realities in the region require that other approaches and concepts be considered as well.

Among the most important of the realities which will confront peacemakers are the following: the Israeli-Palestinian confrontation has now come to the fore as the most urgent and complex

3

part of the Arab-Israeli conflict; demographic trends provide a strong incentive to Israelis to reach an agreement with their Palestinian neighbors which will keep Israel secure, democratic, and predominantly Jewish; the idea of a settlement with Israel is no longer a taboo in the Arab world; and the Soviet Union is becoming more active in the region.

3. The American Role

We would like to see a steady, high-level commitment of American resources to the Arab-Israeli peace process. American leadership can help to create the atmosphere in which negotiations can take place. The United States can also assist in bridging differences on both procedural and substantive issues.

Given the prolonged stalemate in the peace process, attention must now be paid to rebuilding the foundations for a negotiated settlement. Since both Israel and the United States will have new governments in place early in 1989, a special effort will be required to develop a relationship of trust if the peace process is to advance. Consultations must take place with other parties as well before a judgment can be made on when and whether the circumstances are ripe for moving into formal negotiations.

4. An International Framework for Negotiations

Convening an international conference on the Arab-Israeli conflict is the most widely supported approach to negotiations. While we have some reservations about such a forum, we believe that the idea should be explored seriously by a new administration. Indeed, the effort to organize a conference could help to precipitate the political decisions necessary to negotiate a settlement. If a conference is convened, it should not impose its views on the negotiating parties or be empowered to veto the results of bilateral negotiations.

On the controversial issue of Palestinian participation, we have concluded that Palestinians should be represented in any negotiations with Israel by spokesmen of their own choosing, whether in a joint Jordanian-Palestinian delegation or in some other configuration. The United States should have no objection to the participation of Palestinians who are on record as being prepared to coexist with the state of Israel, are committed to peaceful negotiations, can contribute to that objective, and renounce the use of force. Palestinians are unlikely to come forward to negotiate with Israel without having the implicit or explicit endorsement of the Palestine Liberation Organization.

5. Basic Principles for Arab-Israeli Peace

We believe the United States should formulate a strategy for promoting Arab-Israeli peace based on the following points:
—In order to achieve broad Arab-Israeli peace, both Israel and the Palestinians must be directly involved.

—A recognition that the area defined as the former mandate of Palestine west of the Jordan River is home to both peoples is essential to a reconciliation between Israelis and Palestinians.

—Israelis and Palestinians will have to work closely with the Hashemite Kingdom of Jordan, a majority of whose citizens are Palestinians, in shaping a peace agreement. Negotiations must encompass the political and economic relationships among the three parties.

—Under international sponsorship, Israel and Syria should be encouraged to negotiate peace based on the principles of U.N. Resolution 242.

6. Transitional Steps

Within these guidelines, we believe that some form of transitional arrangements must be part of the next phase of Arab-Israeli peacemaking. The atmosphere for peacemaking would be significantly improved by the following sorts of steps, some of which could either precede formal negotiations or be part of an interim agreement:
—ceasing all forms of violence;
—ending the state of belligerency and economic and diplomatic boycott between Israel and its Arab neighbors;

5

—minimizing the Israeli military presence in populated areas of the West Bank and Gaza;

—placing substantial authority in the hands of West Bank and Gaza Palestinians, especially with respect to land, water, economic activity, and political organization; and

—halting new Israeli settlements and land expropriation in the occupied territories.

The United States should also support free elections to municipal councils as an essential step that would allow Palestinians to select their own leaders for purposes of self-government and as possible participants in a Palestinian negotiating delegation.

For Palestinians to find merit in them, these interim measures must be seen as part of an ongoing process that leads to negotiation of a comprehensive peace that meets Palestinian political aspirations. For Israelis to support them, they must be compatible with Israel's assessment of its security interests and be judged as having intrinsic merit.

A transitional arrangement should also be negotiated for the Golan Heights that would enhance mutual security there, return territory to Syria, and establish a new relationship of nonbelligerency as a step toward an overall peace settlement.

7. A Long-Term Vision of Peace

We believe the United States is uniquely positioned to articulate a vision of how Israelis, Palestinians, and other Arab parties can attain their rights to security and to self-determination through a political formula based on ideas of peaceful interchange, political pluralism, and the exchange of "territory for peace" as envisaged in U.N. Resolution 242. Federal or confederal arrangements that would reflect distinctive national identities, while at the same time permitting political and economic linkages among the individual political units, might be an appealing formula.

We envision a future in which borders would not be physical barriers; citizens of one political entity could live safely, and with recognized rights, elsewhere in the region; and economic transactions and movement of individuals would be subject to few restrictions. A regional economic plan with international support should complement such a political settlement and help to ensure its viability.

Jerusalem will be internationally recognized as Israel's capital under any future peace agreements. But Jerusalem is the center of Palestinian aspirations as well. Therefore, a peaceful Jerusalem should remain a unified city, with guaranteed freedom of worship and access, and political arrangements should be found that reflect the nature of the city's population.

Finally, we want to emphasize that the details of an Arab-Israeli peace settlement should not be dictated by the United States or any other outside party. From the standpoint of American interests, the important point is that any agreement be durable. The United States will doubtless benefit by a widening of the scope of Arab-Israeli peace. How that is done is less important than that it be done, and that the process start soon.

THE REPORT

Introduction

ARAB-ISRAELI PEACEMAKING deserves to be high on the agenda of the next American administration. A prolonged impasse in the peace process could endanger U.S. national interests. Recent violent clashes between Israelis and Palestinians are vivid reminders of the explosive situation in the region. For the moment, they appear to have compounded the problem of how to bring about a process of negotiation.

Palestinian leaders in the West Bank and Gaza may feel that these violent demonstrations have served their purposes, especially in influencing international and Israeli public opinion. This may explain their unwillingness to begin a negotiating process that might curtail these demonstrations. Israeli leaders, even those most positively disposed toward negotiations, may find the present moment inopportune because they fear that an agreement to negotiate now would be perceived as weakness and capitulation to violence. Nonetheless, these clashes may reawaken in all parties a recognition of the critical need to renew the Arab-Israeli peace process. Possible openings toward peace have also been created by other regional and international developments. In sum, major obstacles to peace exist, but so do opportunities for diplomacy.

The United States has contributed significantly to Arab-Israeli peace in the past. We believe that it can and should do so again. The stalemate has lasted too long and is too deeply rooted to be overcome easily. More will be required than simply calling on the parties to the conflict to enter into negotiations. The need now is for a politically realistic strategy of peacemaking that concentrates on rebuilding the foundations for a major diplomatic effort.

A new administration should recognize from the outset that advancing the cause of Arab-Israeli peace, while challenging and complex, is necessary if American interests in the region are to be protected. Policymaking by fits and starts is bound to fail. Only a sustained and sustainable diplomatic strategy can produce positive results.

Arguments for inaction are familiar: the conflict is so intractable that no third party can hope to resolve it; it is better to let the pressures in the region build in order to create a more propitious atmosphere for diplomacy; the known, if imperfect, status quo is preferable to a risky, unknown alternative; the struggle between Arabs and Israelis has in recent years receded in importance for Arab governments and for a world preoccupied by other issues. Arguably, these perspectives justify an aloof American stance. We do not agree.

We believe it is imperative to restore a sense of possibility to the search for Arab-Israeli peace and to communicate that sense clearly to the American public and to the parties to the conflict. A reinvigorated Arab-Israeli peace process can serve American interests. American leadership in the Middle East, already strengthened by recent measures taken in the Gulf, can be further enhanced. Israel's peace with Egypt can be deepened and complemented by peace with other Arab parties. Success cannot be guaranteed, of course, but our assessment of risks and opportunities leads us to conclude that the effort is worthwhile.

There is no need to dwell at length on why the United States should care about the Arab-Israeli conflict. The traditional list of American interests in the Middle East—concern for Soviet inroads, the danger of a war that could draw in the superpowers, the special relationship with Israel, support for moderate Arab regimes, access to the region and its resources—are all still relevant. But though U.S. interests remain constant, regional realities are undergoing rapid change. The United States can no longer protect its interests simply by replaying policies from the past.

Several distinct dangers to American interests emanate from the continuing Arab-Israeli conflict. One involves the risk of a large war between Syria and Israel. Both nations are heavily armed with conventional and unconventional weapons. Each is backed by a superpower. Conflict between them, while not imminent, is a continuing possibility, and it could risk U.S.-Soviet confrontation, the avoidance of which is a vital U.S. interest. Averting Syrian-Israeli conflict will require a serious American dialogue with Syria and the Soviet Union; attentiveness to military developments on the Syrian-Israeli front and in Lebanon; and a diplomatic strategy that holds open the door for both Israel and Syria to develop greater mutual security and peaceful relations.

A second danger involves the continuing conflict between Israel and the Palestinians. This conflict is the source of violence and bloodshed, especially in the West Bank and Gaza. It is an unavoidable issue in the U.S.-Israeli dialogue. Along with the broader Arab-Israeli conflict, the Palestinian issue affects U.S. relations with many Arab countries, often making it difficult to develop and maintain broad security relations, especially with Jordan and the Gulf states.

The present relationship between Israel and the Palestinians is neither desirable nor stable, as the violent clashes in late 1987 and early 1988 have amply demonstrated. The military occupation imposes heavy costs on Palestinians who live under it. Israeli society has not escaped the pernicious effects of exercising the power of a military occupier over a prolonged period.

The occupation has deepened antipathy between Israelis and Palestinians, creating an atmosphere of fear, continuing violence, and hardening of attitudes, especially among Israeli and Palestinian youth. Jordan is also an involved party because of its concern that any severe deterioration in the present situation could adversely affect its security.

Some voices in Israel and in the Arab world are recasting the

13

conflict in religious and ideological terms. Palestinian and Israeli extremists confront one another with grim pictures of the future, while moderate voices seek reconciliation based on the idea of a historic compromise between the two claimants to the same land. Those who are using the language of realism and pragmatism to discuss possible ways out of the impasse have developed a range of potentially important contacts. These discussions across the political divide could provide part of the foundation for a revived peace process.

The United States, deeply involved with Israel and committed to basic principles of peace and justice, cannot be indifferent to the Israeli-Palestinian conflict and its broader regional ramifications. It is an engaged party. The question is what role it will choose to play.

Adding to the urgency of addressing the Arab-Israeli conflict is the protracted Gulf war between Iran and Iraq, which has profound regional implications. If Iran were to prevail in the war, many Arab regimes would feel threatened; religiously based extremism could be expected to grow; and the chances for an Arab-Israeli peace based on accommodation and mutual recognition would evaporate.

Yet another reason for concern stems from the U.S.-Egyptian-Israeli triangular relationship. The central pillar of the U.S. position in the region for the past decade, this relationship must be carefully tended. For the moment, it remains firm, but there are obvious strains. Egypt has reestablished normal relations with most of its Arab neighbors, a development viewed with ambivalence and some suspicion by Israelis, who seek assurances that their treaty with Egypt will result in real peace and full normalization of relations. But that seems unlikely unless and until there is progress toward a broader Arab-Israeli peace.

Egypt has always insisted that its peace with Israel was not achieved at the expense of Palestinian rights and that its ties to the United States and Israel can help advance the cause of Arab-Israeli peace. When there is no movement in the peace process, or when Israeli-Palestinian confrontations take place, the Egyptian regime comes under mounting domestic and Arab pressures to curtail its dealings with Israel. Any sharp deterioration of Egyptian-Israeli relations, as occurred after the 1982 war in

Lebanon, could also quickly undermine U.S.-Egyptian ties and sharply set back U.S. interests in the region.

All of these considerations support the case for a broadly defined peace strategy. Time is of the essence. It may still be possible to lay some of the foundation for a sustained peace effort in the remainder of 1988. In any event, an early start in the new presidential term will be needed because peacemaking will take a long time.

New Realities in the Region

A NEWLY ELECTED PRESIDENT will find some useful building blocks in past American-supported formulations on how to deal with the Arab-Israeli conflict. U.N. Security Council Resolutions 242 and 338, the Camp David Accords, and President Ronald Reagan's proposal of September 1, 1982, for example, embody important principles such as the exchange of "territory for peace," the establishment of "secure and recognized boundaries," negotiations between the parties concerned "under appropriate auspices," "transitional arrangements for the West Bank and Gaza," "solving the Palestinian problem in all its aspects," and a suggestion that the West Bank and Gaza should ultimately be associated in some way with Jordan.

But the next administration cannot simply string these formulations together and call the result a serious policy. Other concepts will have to be considered, and other approaches crafted, in order to reflect new realities in the region. We believe the most important of these realities to be the following:

—*The peace treaty signed between Egypt and Israel in March 1979 has been in force for nearly a decade.* It has not yet fulfilled the most far-reaching hopes for a normal range of bilateral social, cultural, and economic ties. It has produced a relationship durable enough to prevent a return to belligerency, though not strong enough to provide much momentum in the search for a broader peace.

Egypt, while certain to be concerned with encouraging further progress in the peace process, cannot be expected to play a

16

central role in future negotiations. The Egyptian leadership does not feel it can speak authoritatively on behalf of the Palestinians. Its primary concern is to see the peace process revived with direct Palestinian participation. Therefore, the main Egyptian role will be to help set the stage for peace talks and to encourage the process from the sidelines, not to participate in the negotiation of the details of agreements.

—*The United States and Israel have a unique relationship that amounts to an unwritten alliance.* It now embraces a wide range of interests, including extensive security cooperation. This relationship has widespread support from the American public and in Congress and is also understood as a fact of life by most parties in the Middle East. Any American administration is obliged by prior commitments and by domestic political realities to elaborate its peacemaking strategy in close consultation with the Israeli government. Because of the depth of the U.S.-Israeli relationship, however, the United States cannot avoid blame for many of Israel's policies in the eyes of most Arabs. This can be a complicating element in U.S.-Arab relations.

—*Israel is deeply divided over the substantive details of a peace settlement, as well as over the appropriate modalities of seeking peace.* Nonetheless, broad agreement currently exists on several points: no return to the 1967 lines; no independent Palestinian state; no negotiations with the Palestine Liberation Organization (PLO); no division of Jerusalem or change in its status as Israel's capital; and support for direct negotiations with Israel's Arab neighbors on a bilateral basis.

The Likud bloc sees a limited version of autonomy for the Palestinians in the West Bank and Gaza as the basis for a long-term settlement. Likud's commitment to keep all of the territory west of the Jordan River under Israeli control, while seeking to increase the Israeli presence in the West Bank and Gaza so as to make their retention by Israel irreversible, is rooted in ideological and security considerations. While upholding Israel's claim to sovereignty over these areas, Likud has stopped short of calling for annexation, since doing so would force it to deal with the political status of the one and one-half million Palestinians living there.

The Labor party has traditionally placed heavy emphasis on security concerns in the West Bank and Gaza. Labor seeks to advance its idea of "territorial compromise" in direct negotiations with Jordan, and recently has shown interest in establishing shared Israeli-Jordanian rule over the West Bank, at least in the form of de facto interim arrangements.

Demographic trends provide one of the most potent arguments for Israelis who favor a negotiated political settlement based on "territorial compromise" and who fear that without such a compromise Israel could become a state that would be neither predominantly Jewish nor democratic. In all the territory now under Israeli control, more Arab than Jewish babies are born each year, meaning that Arabs may eventually become a majority. Even short of becoming a majority, the Arabs are now, and will continue to be, a large and problematic minority, raising acutely for Jewish Israelis the dilemmas of democratic enfranchisement for Arabs.

For many Israelis, a smaller but more Jewish Israel would be preferred to either the status quo or a large, binational Israel— provided, of course, that such an Israel could live in peace with its Arab neighbors. Likud and its allies are less worried by the demographic argument. They believe that the trends are not irreversible, and that in any case the Arabs can be given political status outside the framework of Israeli politics.

—Several developments raise serious doubts about the feasibility today of a straightforward "territory for peace" deal in the West Bank and Gaza as envisaged in U.N. Resolution 242. The concept of the partition of the land west of the Jordan River into two homelands, one for the Jews and one for the Palestinian Arabs, has never been the subject of serious negotiations between the concerned parties. When the West Bank and Gaza were controlled by Jordan and Egypt, respectively, the Arabs refused to negotiate directly with Israel. After Israel occupied these territories in 1967, the initial Arab response was to reject the idea of peace and direct negotiations with Israel. Later, those Arab governments that accepted U.N. Resolution 242 took the position that negotiations within an international forum could begin only if full Israeli withdrawal to the 1967 lines was assured at

the outset. Israel rejected these terms, calling instead for face-to-face negotiations without preconditions.

In the absence of negotiations, Israel consolidated its own presence in the occupied territories, primarily through the creation of settlements and expropriation of lands. The Likud government that came to power in 1977 made it clear that it no longer interpreted Resolution 242 as requiring any withdrawal from the West Bank, even in exchange for full peace with its neighbors. The Labor party, by contrast, has continued to speak of "territorial compromise," without defining the practical meaning of this formulation in advance of negotiations.

Israelis, Palestinians, and Jordanians have become deeply entangled in one another's affairs during the more than twenty years that Israel has controlled the West Bank, Gaza, and East Jerusalem. Economic interrelationships are now a fact of life and could, in conditions of greater equality, be transformed into positive elements of any peace accord. What has not developed, however, is any mutually acceptable formula that provides a political expression for Palestinian national identity. Nor is there an agreed basis for coexistence, mutual recognition, and security between Israelis and Palestinians. And Israel has still not won recognition, acceptance, and full peace from its Arab neighbors.

While some of the new contacts between Israelis and Palestinians may ultimately help pave the way for peace, other developments raise questions about how the territorial dimension of a compromise can be worked out under present conditions. For example, Israeli law has been extended to East Jerusalem and to the Golan Heights. Some 65,000 Israeli settlers now have their homes in the West Bank, as do several thousand more in Gaza and Golan, along with another 100,000 or more who live in and around East Jerusalem in territory formerly subject to Jordanian rule.

From the Palestinian side, there has generally been a reluctance to state clearly that peace with Israel could be achieved if Israel were to withdraw to specified lines on the map. While PLO officials have spoken of a Palestinian state in the West Bank and Gaza and have indicated a willingness to accept "all relevant U.N. resolutions, including 242 and 338," some in the

PLO still call for a solution to the Palestinian problem in stages, implying that even if Israel were to withdraw to the 1967 lines, the conflict would continue until the Jewish state was dismantled. For a large majority of Israelis, these Palestinian positions, along with the perception of the PLO as an organization wedded to the use of terror, confirm their suspicion that the PLO's ultimate goal is the destruction of Israel, and they therefore refuse to do anything that might legitimize such an organization.

Meanwhile, for a whole generation of Israelis and Palestinians, the "green line" that had effectively separated their two societies from 1949 until 1967 has lost much of its earlier meaning, even though the political and cultural divide continues to be very real. Although in normal times some 100,000 Palestinians cross this line every day to work in Israel, there is still little real integration or cooperation between the two societies and peoples.

As the stalemate has continued with little hope of change, the Palestinian demand for a state has grown ever louder. Palestinian nationalism has gained in strength in the past twenty years. Palestinians are unwilling to subordinate their identity within the larger framework of Arabism, or to entrust their fate to the existing Arab regimes. Israeli Arabs are now conscious of their identity as Palestinians, even as they are increasingly assertive as a force in Israeli politics. Within the West Bank and Gaza, and certainly among Palestinians elsewhere as well, the PLO has become widely accepted as the primary symbol of Palestinian national aspirations, even by those who disagree with specific policies and actions or who criticize its leaders.

In brief, the past twenty years have resulted in a blurring of some of the differences between pre-1967 Israel and the West Bank and Gaza. In other respects, however, the dividing lines between the two societies remain clear. These contradictory patterns severely complicate any simple application of the "territory for peace" formula of U.N. Resolution 242, while raising questions about the feasibility of other formulations as well.

—*Peace with Israel is still a contentious issue in Arab domestic politics, although the Palestinian issue is no longer invariably at the*

20

top of the inter-Arab agenda. Although most Arab regimes are on record as favoring some form of settlement, no such consensus exists at the popular level, where divisions are sharp over the terms for peace, and even over its desirability. As a result, Arab political leaders who might favor accommodation with Israel are reluctant to move in that direction. This hesitancy has been particularly evident since the rise of Islamic political movements that tend to redefine the conflict in absolutist terms.

Nonetheless, there is some room for flexibility, in part because Arab governments are preoccupied by other issues, such as economic problems, the Iran-Iraq war, and demands for greater political participation and democratization. In this atmosphere, Arab rejection of coexistence with Israel has been in retreat. Peace with Israel may not have a wide constituency in the Arab world, but the idea of reaching a formal settlement with Israel is no longer taboo within the mainstream of the Arab world. This mainstream, however, remains cautious and skeptical, and a bold initiative such as former Egyptian president Anwar Sadat's trip to Jerusalem is therefore highly unlikely in today's environment.

—The PLO has maintained a two-track policy in recent years. It continues to call for "armed struggle" against Israel. At the same time, the dominant group within the PLO has developed a political program calling for self-determination leading to an independent Palestinian state west of the Jordan River in any area to be evacuated by Israel, an immediate end to Israeli military occupation of the West Bank and Gaza, and the representation of the PLO, directly or indirectly, in any peace negotiations. Until the United States recognizes the right of the Palestinians to self-determination, the PLO refuses to make what it considers to be unilateral concessions, such as unconditionally accepting U.N. Resolution 242.

Some Palestinians, both within and outside the PLO, adopt a more extreme line of refusing negotiations of any sort with Israel. They call for a military solution, and openly espouse the dismantling of Israel as a predominantly Jewish state and its replacement by a "democratic state" in all of the former Palestine mandate west of the Jordan River.

—Syria has accepted U.N. Resolutions 242 and 338 with the interpretation that they call for full Israeli withdrawal from all occupied territories and Palestinian self-determination. Were its interpretation of these resolutions to be accepted and implemented, the Syrian regime has said that it would enter into a nonbelligerency agreement with Israel, but has ruled out the more expansive idea of normalization of relations and full peace treaties. Syria wants to be involved in any efforts to resolve the Palestinian issue and will not readily agree to limit its role to bilateral negotiations with Israel over the Golan. Because the Syrian regime fears isolation and strongly opposes separate deals, it insists on an international conference with real powers reserved for the plenary sessions. It also seems to favor a high-level dialogue with the United States, especially as its relationship with the Soviet Union has come under some strain.

Syria is pursuing the goal of achieving ''strategic parity'' with Israel in order to have an independent military option in the event of another war with Israel and as a necessary precondition for any negotiations. Syria also continues to support Palestinian groups that take a strongly rejectionist posture on the issue of peace with Israel.

President Hafiz al-Asad always plays his cards close to the chest, so it is impossible to know exactly where the main line of Syrian policy is headed or how Syria's attitudes might be affected if a serious peace initiative was to get under way. There are, however, some signs of change toward a more flexible posture on a number of issues, including a decrease in support for extremist Palestinian groups and a more balanced policy toward the Gulf conflict. The impossibility of reaching real strategic parity with Israel anytime in the foreseeable future also seems to be understood by many Syrians. In addition, Syria continues to respect the terms of the 1974 disengagement agreement with Israel and has had informal security understandings with Israel in Lebanon in the past.

—Under General Secretary Mikhail Gorbachev, the Soviet position toward the Arab-Israeli conflict has become more activist and less rigid than in the 1970s. The Soviets have consistently supported U.N. Resolutions 242 and 338 and Israel's right to exist as an

independent Jewish state. But in the past this position has been coupled with strong anti-Zionist rhetoric, along with support for the Arab interpretation of Israel's obligation to withdraw from all occupied territory and to allow the Palestinians to form a state of their own. More recently, the Soviets have reestablished a dialogue with Israel and have undertaken a number of initiatives with the Arab parties to the conflict. They have pressed for both PLO unity and PLO-Syrian rapprochement.

The primary Soviet objective seems to be to ensure that no negotiations take place outside the framework of a Soviet-supported international conference. While being very insistent on the principle of a conference, however, the Soviets have hinted at considerable flexibility on the modalities of negotiating. For example, they seem prepared to accept the idea of a Jordanian-Palestinian delegation at a conference, and so may not insist on separate PLO participation. In essence, the Soviets argue that there must be parallel movement on the Syrian and Palestinian fronts—and that Soviet participation is essential to progress in both these arenas.

A Strategy for Peacemaking

IN THE PAST DECADE AND A HALF, the American approach to the Arab-Israeli conflict has spanned the spectrum from intense involvement at the highest level to passivity and neglect. To some extent the choice was dictated by circumstances. But it also reflected different philosophical stances toward the peace process, evident in at least three schools of thought.

One approach, closely identified with former Secretary of State Henry Kissinger in the 1969–73 period, argued for an aloof stance until the right set of regional circumstances presented themselves. Then in 1974–75, in the aftermath of the October 1973 Arab-Israeli war, Kissinger recommended active, high-level involvement, aimed at persuading Middle East leaders to rethink their positions within a strategic political framework and to move step-by-step toward agreements. Both President Richard Nixon and Kissinger believed that regional crises often created opportunities for imaginative diplomacy. This belief was not an argument for creating such crises, but it did mean that American officials were most prone to become active when the status quo had been jolted by a sudden shock.

President Jimmy Carter and his secretary of state, Cyrus Vance, followed a second approach. They also were proponents of an active American role in the Arab-Israeli peace process but were less inclined than Nixon and Kissinger to wait for propitious regional circumstances. They argued that it was too dangerous to wait until a crisis created new opportunities for diplomacy. Instead, they felt that American leadership could bring about

24

significant change in the positions of the parties and could help to establish an agreed set of principles to guide negotiations toward a successful conclusion.

President Reagan and Secretary of State George Shultz have, on the whole, adopted yet another approach, preferring that the United States not commit its resources to Arab-Israeli diplomacy until the parties to the conflict are clearly ready for serious negotiations. They have been concerned about raising expectations too high by holding out the prospect of an active American role. The more the parties came to depend on Washington, they believed, the less they would be prepared to deal directly with one another.

The Reagan administration has encouraged Jordan and Israel to engage in direct negotiations, with Palestinians represented as junior partners under Jordan's tutelage. To that end, it has been prepared to explore the ideas of an international conference, of U.S.-Soviet sponsorship of direct negotiations, and of autonomy for the West Bank and Gaza as an interim step toward an overall settlement. Until recently, Arab-Israeli peacemaking has received only sporadic presidential attention during the Reagan years.

We believe the next president should draw on some elements of policy from the approaches of each of his predecessors. He would be prudent to promise no more than can be delivered, to keep pressure on the parties to do as much as they can on their own, and to be alert to events that might provide new opportunities for peacemaking. Yet he must also set a new priority and a new tone for his Middle East policy by signaling that the United States has a continuing interest of its own in seeing the conflict settled and by making the command decisions that will be needed to place the Arab-Israeli conflict high on his foreign-policy agenda. His approach will need to be articulated in ways that enlist congressional and public support for his diplomacy of peacemaking. He will have to be especially attentive to his administration's political calendar, for if he puts aside Arab-Israeli issues for too long, he may run out of time, dissipating the advantages of early diplomatic movement.

The steady, high-level commitment of resources that we urge should avoid vacillation between passivity and activism in America's Arab-Israeli diplomacy. There is less need for bold new initiatives than for an ongoing political dialogue, sustained and energetic involvement, and a conscious wedding of American power to the purposes of the diplomacy of peace. Much can be done through the imaginative use of existing diplomatic channels, provided that the secretary of state is himself directly engaged. The president's role, accordingly, can be properly kept in reserve, enabling him to serve more as a concerned and knowledgeable "court of last resort" on the difficult issues than as "desk officer" for the day-to-day negotiations.

The United States cannot, by itself, reinvigorate Arab-Israeli peacemaking, but what it says and does will have a substantial influence on the views of all the parties and on the eventual agenda for negotiations. The overall posture that we urge would require a series of political discussions with all the concerned parties as early as possible.

Much of what we are recommending should be seen as the essence of diplomacy. But conventional diplomacy is never quite enough in dealing with Arab-Israeli issues. So thoroughly politicized and so complex are these issues that they call for a skillful strategy to cope with the competing claims of Arabs and Israelis, with the pull of constituents and members of Congress who care deeply about the Middle East, and with the obligations undertaken by previous administrations, especially those obligations that have evolved from the development of the special relationship with Israel.

To address the competing claims on the domestic front, the administration will need to work to ensure that Congress and the American public understand, and share in, the broad purposes of its Arab-Israeli peace diplomacy. Significant benefits can be derived if the administration seeks an active partnership with Congress in the search for Middle East peace. The valuable experience of members of Congress who have dealt with Arab-Israeli issues over the years could be tapped. An informed congressional constituency could help to promote policies based on long-term strategic considerations.

Evidence from public opinion surveys shows that American

citizens would strongly support a U.S.-led peace initiative. They took great pride in the role their government played in brokering peace between Egypt and Israel, and they would no doubt do so again if the United States was helpful in bringing about reconciliation between Israel and its Palestinian and other Arab neighbors.

As the first order of business, the United States will need to help rebuild the foundations of the peace process. That requires a sense of strategy, a series of connected moves informed by a clear political purpose, and a recognition that choices do exist. Peacemaking has been stalled too long for small steps taken outside of a wider political framework to lead very far.

Given Israel's sense of international isolation, vulnerability, and dependence on the United States, the president can make a key contribution to this broader framework by conveying to the Israeli leadership and public that he shares with Congress a personal commitment to the U.S.-Israeli relationship and to Israel's security. If the president gains Israel's trust early on in his administration, the prospects for winning Israeli acceptance of an active American role in the peace process will be enhanced. Gaining that trust can best be done if the president takes a personal interest in the conduct of the relationship, meets directly with Israeli leaders, engages in serious private discussions of the peace process before taking public initiatives, and reaffirms that economic and security relationships will be maintained.

With traditional Arab friends—especially Egypt and Jordan— the need is for close consultations on how best to revive the peace process. A wide range of useful steps can be discussed that could substantially improve the atmosphere for negotiations. To be effective, talks with both Israeli and Arab leaders cannot just be fact-finding missions. They must actively identify the obstacles to negotiations and begin building a common approach to removing them.

It is not enough, however, to talk only with traditional friends. Syria has for too long been treated as either irrelevant to the peace process or beyond the reach of diplomacy. But Syria has the capacity to complicate or thwart the negotiating efforts if ignored, as amply shown from 1982 to 1987. A high-level dialogue between Washington and Damascus is needed to determine whether and how Syria is prepared to contribute to the peace process. The United States should be open to a fundamental improvement in its relationship with Syria. It would have to be understood that such an improvement could not take place if Syria was to support international terrorism or actively obstruct the peace process. Absent these obstacles, however, the United States should be prepared to discuss Arab-Israeli diplomacy and other regional issues with Damascus.

The United States will also need to find ways to consult at this early stage with representative Palestinians. Numerous channels for direct and indirect communication exist, even within the strictures set by current law, and efforts should be made to use them effectively to persuade authoritative Palestinian leaders that they have an incentive to support the next phase of peacemaking.

The United States also needs to consider how best to discuss Arab-Israeli diplomacy with the Soviet Union. U.S.-Soviet relations have entered a phase of serious dialogue on a wide range of issues, first and foremost on strategic arms control. The Arab-Israeli conflict has moved higher on the superpower agenda and should remain there. The United States and the Soviet Union do not have identical interests in the region, but they share a concern for the consequences of another large-scale war, which might draw them into a direct confrontation. In addition, both countries should be worried about the possibility of an erosion of commitment to a peaceful settlement of the Arab-Israeli conflict and a growth of political and religious extremism.

The Need for an International Framework

DESPITE U.S. AND ISRAELI CALLS for face-to-face negotiations between Israel and Jordan, King Hussein has insisted on an international framework for negotiations. His insistence has generated considerable discussion of the possibility of convening an international conference. Jordan, Egypt, part of the Israeli government, most Palestinians, Syria, the Soviet Union, and the United States have all expressed support for some form of international conference, even though views differ widely on details. American and Soviet diplomats, moreover, have discussed many of the details associated with an international conference.

This history should not be swept aside by a new administration. The effort to organize a conference could by itself help to precipitate the political decisions necessary to negotiate a settlement. For this and other reasons, we believe that a new administration should weigh seriously the issues associated with convening an international conference. The first priority is to create a political atmosphere in which the parties to the conflict will be encouraged to negotiate. Since bilateral negotiations by themselves appear to be unacceptable to Jordan, Syria, and the Palestinians, some other formula will be needed to bring about direct negotiations. An international framework that ensures both participation in the negotiations by the key regional parties and a degree of international support for the effort seems to be called for.

29

Certain conditions should be met before the United States commits itself to a specific formula for reviving negotiations within an international framework. First, the parties to the conflict will have to accept the formula. Second, the United States and the Soviet Union should be in broad agreement on procedures. Third, some points of substance should already have been discussed with the negotiating parties so that negotiations can proceed from a common agenda. Extensive political dialogue will be needed to establish whether these conditions have been met.

In supporting U.N. Resolution 338, the United States endorsed the concept of negotiations "between the parties concerned under appropriate auspices" as the best way to resolve the Arab-Israeli conflict. This is a suitably vague, yet useful, formula, and it was clearly understood at the time that it meant U.S.-Soviet auspices for the negotiations.

A further prerequisite should be satisfied before the United States presses for the convening of an international conference. Four procedural issues must be answered in ways that protect American interests and facilitate negotiations.

Who will represent the Palestinians?

What role will the Soviet Union play?

What will be the authority of the plenary with respect to any agreements reached bilaterally?

How can all parties, and especially the Syrians, be given a stake in the conference, without at the same time having a veto over its outcome?

A realistic assessment of current prospects for an international conference should assume that Israel will not alter its position of refusing to negotiate with the PLO and that the PLO will continue its policy of using all means, including violence, to achieve its goals. Perhaps these assumptions will prove wrong; if so, the problem of getting Israelis and Palestinians to talk to one another may be eased. For the time being, however, the gap between Israel and the PLO will be difficult to bridge.

Some have argued that Jordan is therefore the logical alternative to the PLO in any negotiations with Israel. King Hussein, however, is reluctant to move into negotiations without Palestinian backing, which is unlikely to be forthcoming unless the PLO gives the green light to its supporters.

We believe that Palestinians should be represented in any negotiations with Israel by spokesmen of their own choosing, whether in a joint Jordanian-Palestinian delegation or in some other configuration. As a general guideline, the United States should have no objection to the participation of Palestinians who are on record as being prepared to coexist with the state of Israel, are committed to peaceful negotiations, can contribute to that objective, and agree to renounce the use of force. In practical terms, we recognize that Palestinians are unlikely to come forward to negotiate with Israel without having the implicit or explicit endorsement of the PLO.

The need for Soviet involvement in this stage of diplomacy is twofold. First, all the Arab parties, including Jordan, Syria, and Egypt, want an international framework that would involve both superpowers. Second, the Soviets have some influence over the positions of Syria and the PLO and have moved toward developing a working relationship with Israel as well. If it were possible to think only in terms of an Israeli-Jordanian bilateral peace negotiation, the Soviet role would not be so important. But since Syria and the Palestinians must be included as well, then the Soviets do have a role to play stemming from their relations with these two parties.

Drawing on earlier precedents from the 1973 Geneva Middle East Peace Conference, which was convened by the secretary general of the United Nations under U.S.-Soviet cochairmanship, neither superpower would directly participate in the formal bilateral negotiations that will take place. The American and Soviet roles will be derived from the nature of their relations with the parties, not from the formal organization of the conference.

The challenge for the United States, we believe, is to pursue negotiations in ways that will give the Soviets incentives to play a constructive role. In addition to consulting with the Soviets on steps the two superpowers could each take to foster the beginning of negotiations and to find an acceptable formula for Palestinian representation, the United States should explore other procedural matters. For example, it will be important to establish the proposition that a peace conference will not be authorized to impose solutions or to veto the results of bilateral negotiations. It is also assumed that the Soviet Union will reestablish normal diplomatic relations with Israel in the context of an international conference.

The role of the plenary sessions of the conference has become controversial. At a minimum, the plenary is needed for the symbolic purpose of starting formal negotiations. To think that there will be no other role for it, as some have maintained, is probably unrealistic. Such issues as refugee claims, peacekeeping arrangements, international guarantees, and future economic programs in the region could be dealt with in a multilateral setting if the negotiating parties were to agree. But the plenary should not be allowed to obstruct the work of direct bilateral negotiations.

The issue of Syrian participation has bedeviled all previous efforts to organize an international conference. Secretary Kissinger spent many hours in 1973 on this matter, only to be told on the eve of the Geneva conference that Syria would not participate. Nonetheless, several months later Syria did sign a disengagement agreement with Israel under the auspices of the Geneva conference. The United States should try to ensure that Syria has an incentive to participate constructively in peace-making.

The United States should make clear its support for negotiations between Israel and Syria on the basis of the principles of U.N. Resolution 242. The United States has not accepted as final Israel's unilateral steps with respect to the Golan Heights, where Israeli law is now applied and settlements have been established. The United States has a primary interest in the stability of the Syrian-Israeli front and should support any peacekeeping measures that will help reduce the danger of war. United Nations peacekeeping forces have played a useful role on this front and can be expected to do so again in any future settlement. This is a strong argument for keeping the United Nations involved from the outset in efforts to organize peace negotiations.

The Syrians want to be assured that their voice will be heard on the Palestinian question. They should understand that the United States will not support a Syrian veto power on this issue, but that Damascus is free to use whatever legitimate political influence it has with the Jordanians and the Palestinians to ensure that its views are taken into account. This is a matter of inter-Arab politics, not of conference procedures.

We do not unreservedly support the idea of an international conference on Arab-Israeli peace. A conference that quickly deadlocked or broke down could raise regional tensions. If better alternatives present themselves along the way, the United States should respond favorably. For the moment, however, no other idea enjoys wide support, and we are convinced that the United States is well positioned to assist in shaping such a conference and to play an effective role.

Negotiating a Transition to Peace

CLEARING THE PROCEDURAL HURDLES on the way to an agreed international framework for negotiations is a necessary but not sufficient component in a new administration's peacemaking strategy. For the regional parties most directly involved, substantive questions are the paramount concerns, and the United States must therefore be prepared to address those questions as its peacemaking strategy evolves.

The United States should not be in the business of drawing up detailed blueprints for a final settlement, which in any case will be rejected out of hand by the parties or treated as irrelevant. Nor, however, can the United States be constructively engaged in the peacemaking process unless its strategy is guided by basic principles concerning the character and content of a peace that Israelis, Palestinians, and other Arabs can regard as viable and just.

The central problem in organizing negotiations is how to avoid at the outset the probable impasse over territorial, juridical, and other issues of a final settlement, while still addressing enough of the principles of a comprehensive peace to bring in those who want assurances that their concerns are part of the negotiating framework. This is a familiar problem in diplomacy and can be dealt with if the United States understands the core requirements of both the Israelis and Palestinians, for they are the two parties at the heart of the conflict today.

We believe the United States can develop a constructive approach to Arab-Israeli peacemaking based on an appreciation of the following points:

—The central historic compromise will have to involve Israel and the Palestinians. It cannot be negotiated over their heads.

—At the same time, the conflict between Israel and its Arab neighbors, especially Syria and Jordan, will require direct negotiations leading to peace treaties.

—Reconciliation between Israelis and Palestinians will have to stem from a recognition that the land consisting of the former mandate of Palestine west of the Jordan River is home to both peoples. Each is entitled to recognition and respect from the other as they negotiate a new peaceful relationship. Each should be able to live in security in this land. Any territorial division that might be negotiated on the basis of the principle of "territory for peace" should allow for agreed economic and social relationships between the two peoples on the basis of equality. These principles could be reflected in a variety of political arrangements to be negotiated between the parties.

—The future of both Israelis and Palestinians is closely intertwined with that of the Hashemite Kingdom of Jordan, more than half of whose citizens are themselves Palestinians. The political and economic relationships among Israelis, Palestinians, and Jordanians must be negotiated.

With these broad guidelines in mind, we believe the next steps in the peace process must concentrate on concrete interim measures that meet the immediate needs of all parties to the conflict, as an integral part of negotiating a final settlement to be embodied in peace treaties. Negotiations will deadlock immediately if the first order of business is defined as drawing up the terms of a final peace. Most of the parties to the conflict recognize that some form of transitional arrangement must be built into the next phase of Arab-Israeli peacemaking.

Both Israelis and Palestinians attach great importance to the issue of "linkage" between interim steps and an overall settlement. The Israelis maintain that it is essential for any transitional arrangement to stand on its own and not be dependent upon subsequent stages of agreement. The Palestinians and other Arab parties seek a much tighter relationship between interim steps and a final settlement.

In the past, the United States has tried to bridge this difference by emphasizing that peacemaking is a process in which the parties must participate if they wish to achieve their goals; it is not a guarantee of a specific outcome in advance. In addition, American administrations have tried to make transitional arrangements acceptable by ensuring that they met the real needs of both sides to the conflict. Finally, the United States has also been willing to hold out a picture of a final settlement and to affirm its readiness to stay the course until a comprehensive peace is reached. All of these points should continue as part of the American approach.

The idea of negotiations on interim steps or transitional arrangements has generally had minimal appeal to Arab parties for two reasons. First, those in the West Bank and Gaza who would be most immediately affected did not see much change from the prevailing situation of occupation; those living elsewhere, meanwhile, suspected a conscious effort to split them from Palestinians in the West Bank and Gaza. Second, the link between the transitional arrangements and an overall agreement was left vague, which raised major questions on the part of all Palestinians and other Arabs.

In view of this history, we conclude that transitional arrangements will win Palestinian support only if they are seen as firmly linked to the principles of an overall settlement. American diplomacy should therefore not only aim to make the transitional arrangements as attractive as possible to the parties in their own right, but also continue to stress that the United States will stay involved beyond the transitional stage to work for a comprehensive peace.

For the Israelis, the merit of transitional arrangements is that Israeli security concerns will be fully protected while new political arrangements are tested. *During a transitional period, Israel should also receive some of the benefits of an overall peace with its Arab neighbors, at a minimum including an end to belligerency and to economic and diplomatic boycotts.* If agreement on a transitional regime for the West Bank and Gaza can be reached through negotiations within an agreed international framework, Israel should be able to enhance its situation internationally and with neighboring states. An agreement would also relieve Israel of some of the problems associated with the demographic challenge. As Palestinians are allowed to develop their own distinctive political institutions, quite possibly in free association with Jordan, and as the current unequal relationship between Israelis and Palestinians is modified, the threat to Israeli principles of democracy posed by the continuing occupation will lessen.

It remains our hope that formal negotiations will be initiated promptly between Israel and its neighbors. We recognize, however, the barriers to such negotiations and are concerned about the dangerously confrontational and violent drift in relations between Israelis and Palestinians. If not reversed, these trends could further reduce the prospect of negotiations ever taking place. Israelis and Palestinians living in the West Bank and Gaza need to consider seriously major changes in the pattern of their day-to-day interactions. Therefore, some of the measures that we would recommend as part of a transitional regime could also be envisaged as steps that the parties could carry out quite apart from formal negotiations.

For example, the atmosphere for peacemaking would be significantly improved by the following sorts of steps: ending all forms of violence; ceasing hostile propaganda; revoking the policy of deportation and collective punishment; placing substantial authority in the hands of West Bank and Gaza Palestinians; and halting the creation of new Israeli settlements and land expropriation in the occupied territories. In addition, the United States should support free elections to municipal councils as an essential step that would allow Palestinians to choose their own leaders for purposes of self-government and as possible participants in a Palestinian negotiating delegation.

For the Palestinians in the West Bank and Gaza, a transitional regime should minimize the Israeli military presence in populated areas of the West Bank and Gaza, and substantially increase Palestinian control over land, water, and economic and political activity. Palestinians must also be able to look forward to normal political rights of self-expression and organization.

Palestinians are unlikely to go along with transitional arrangements unless they are seen as leading to a final settlement that will meet broader Palestinian political aspirations. If that condition is met, then representative Palestinians, wherever they may reside, might be willing to enter direct talks with Israel on interim measures. Similarly, Israelis will be unwilling to enter into new arrangements unless they are seen as compatible with Israel's security and are judged as having intrinsic merit, regardless of whether or not they lead to further steps. If these conditions are met, the Israeli government is likely to agree to negotiate transitional arrangements.

Syria also has something to gain from participating in the peacemaking process. It should have an opportunity to negotiate for new arrangements on the Golan Heights that could enhance mutual security and return territory there to Syrian control. In return, Syria should be prepared to enter into a nonbelligerency agreement or its equivalent. The serious purposes to be served by such arrangements would be to engage Israel and Syria in the negotiating process; to reduce the danger of surprise attack; to provide a forum in which other issues could be usefully discussed; to dissuade the Syrians from trying to block progress on other negotiating fronts; and to create a framework for the improvement of U.S.-Syrian relations.

A Long-Term Vision

While we are convinced that negotiations have to be carefully prepared and should focus in the first instance on two sets of transitional arrangements, one for the West Bank and Gaza and one for the Golan, we also recognize the need for a link between interim agreements and a vision of what lies ahead. There is a place for an American vision of the future in which Israelis and Palestinians, as well as Jordanians, Syrians, and Lebanese, can coexist peacefully, each with a firm political identity and genuine security. If such coexistence could be achieved, it would significantly strengthen the peace between Egypt and Israel as well. We believe, therefore, that it is useful to articulate one possible future that the United States, in good conscience, could support and that would take into account the basic positions of the parties to the conflict.

An appealing model of the future might include federal or confederal arrangements that would reflect distinctive national identities, while providing for political as well as economic linkages among the individual political units. In this vision of the future, borders would not be physical barriers; citizens of one political entity could live safely, and with recognized rights, elsewhere in the region; and economic transactions and movement of individuals would be subject to few restrictions.

We do not have in mind an exact formula for the future that can be applied in the Israeli-Palestinian-Jordanian triangle. We do see, however, a requirement for a political framework that captures what is unique for each people and gives it political expression, while at the same time recognizing a community of interests, a network of interrelationships based on equality, and security arrangements that preclude threats and the use of force in resolving differences. In addition, peace treaties should be signed and normal relations established between Israel and each of its neighbors.

Jerusalem will be internationally recognized as Israel's capital under any future peace arrangements. But Jerusalem is the center of Palestinian political aspirations as well. Therefore, a peaceful Jerusalem should remain a unified city, with guaranteed freedom of worship and access, and political arrangements should be found that reflect the nature of the city's population. Such a Jerusalem, holy to three great religions, could be a meeting place for Jews, Christians, and Muslims.

A vision of a desirable economic future is also needed as a complement to this political framework. Certainly the parties to the conflict should know that serious steps toward peace will be supported by the United States, as well as by others in the international community. They should also recognize that a major benefit of peace will be the availability of resources for domestic purposes that are now devoted to preparations for war. To help realize the economic potential of the region at peace, a major economic development plan should be organized, with the United States, Europe, and Japan taking the lead, and with contributions from others in the Middle East as well. Talk of a "Marshall Plan" for the Middle East in the absence of peace has thus far been little more than rhetoric; with peace it could become a reality.

A tragic byproduct of the wars that have swept the region in the past forty years has been the large numbers of refugees and displaced persons, both Arabs and Jews. As part of any overall settlement, their internationally recognized claims and legitimate grievances should be addressed. Those refugees who are unable to return to their homes should nonetheless be able to secure their future with generous compensation and their own political identity. Here again the international community should help.

Conclusion

WE HAVE A RELATIVELY simple message, but if taken seriously it will involve a difficult, challenging diplomatic task. Our first point is that the Arab-Israeli conflict deserves high priority. The "peace process" needs to be activated and sustained. American leadership is essential for that to happen.

Initially, the American effort should focus on building solid foundations through dialogue with all the interested parties. For serious negotiations to begin, we believe there will be a need for international sponsorship. It will be essential to include the Soviet Union and the U.N. secretary general in the preliminary consultations and in the structuring of an acceptable international setting for negotiations. An international conference makes sense only when and if it can advance the prospects for agreement. That can only be determined through intensive talks with all of the concerned parties.

When negotiations begin, it will be necessary to have in mind an attainable near-term target, as well as an idea of the process for moving from interim agreements to a final settlement. We believe the initial focus of peacemaking should be on transitional arrangements, both for the West Bank and Gaza and for the Golan Heights. Such arrangements should help to create the political climate in which formal peace treaties can eventually be negotiated.

We also believe that the United States is uniquely positioned to articulate a future vision of how Israelis, Palestinians, and other Arab parties can attain their rights to security and to self-

41

determination through a political formula based on ideas of peaceful interchange and political pluralism, and the exchange of "territory for peace" as envisaged in U.N. Resolution 242. Concepts of federation or confederation, respect for minority rights, economic development, and principles of democratic governance are all potential building blocks for a just, lasting, and genuine peace settlement.

Finally, we want to emphasize that the details of an Arab-Israeli peace settlement should not be dictated by the United States or any other outside party. Working out the terms of an agreement is up to the parties who will have to live with the results of negotiations. It is the durability of any agreement that should be foremost in the minds of Americans. U.S. interests, we have no doubt, will be well served by widening the scope of Arab-Israeli peace. How that is done is less important than that it be done, and that the process start soon.

MEMBERS
OF THE STUDY GROUP

ALFRED LEROY ATHERTON, JR.

The Harkness Fellowships of the Commonwealth Fund
Ambassador Atherton was Assistant Secretary of State for Near Eastern and South Asian Affairs from 1974 to 1978; Ambassador-at-Large for Middle East negotiations in 1978–79; and Ambassador to Egypt from 1979 to 1983. He participated in Arab-Israeli peace efforts during 1969–77 and in the Egyptian-Israeli peace negotiations during 1978–79.

HERMANN FREDERICK EILTS

Boston University
Ambassador Eilts is Distinguished University Professor of International Relations and Director of the Center for International Relations at Boston University. He is former Ambassador to Egypt and to Saudi Arabia. He participated in all phases of the Egyptian-Israeli peace negotiations from 1973 to 1979.

LARRY L. FABIAN

Secretary, Carnegie Endowment for International Peace
Mr. Fabian was Director of the Carnegie Endowment's Middle East program in the 1970s. He is the coeditor of *Israelis Speak: About Themselves and the Palestinians*.

Institutional affiliations are noted only for purposes of identification.

DAVID M. GORDIS

Wilstein Institute, University of Judaism

Dr. Gordis is Director of the Wilstein Institute on Public Policy and Vice President of the University of Judaism, Los Angeles, California. He has served as Vice President of the Jewish Theological Seminary of America and Executive Vice President of the American Jewish Committee. He was founding Executive Director of the Foundation for Conservative Judaism in Israel. He has written widely on Middle East matters, on the American Jewish community and its relationship to Israel, and on other areas of American and American Jewish public policy.

RITA E. HAUSER

Senior Partner, Stroock & Stroock & Lavan

Mrs. Hauser is an international lawyer; a founder and member of the Executive Committee, The International Center for Peace in the Middle East; and a former U.S. Representative to the United Nations Commission on Human Rights.

PAUL JABBER

Senior Fellow, Council on Foreign Relations

Mr. Jabber directs the Middle East program at the Council on Foreign Relations. In 1975–82 he taught international relations at the University of California at Los Angeles, and since 1982 he has been responsible for Middle East country risk assessment at Bankers Trust of New York. His latest book is *Not by War Alone: Security and Arms Control in the Middle East.*

GERI M. JOSEPH

Hubert H. Humphrey Institute of Public Affairs

Ambassador Joseph is a Senior Fellow at the Humphrey Institute of Public Affairs. A former journalist and political activist, she has had a long-time interest in Middle East issues. She served as Ambassador to The Netherlands from 1978 to 1981.

RASHID I. KHALIDI

Associate Professor of Modern Middle East History, University of Chicago

Professor Khalidi, a Palestinian American, has taught at the American University of Beirut and at Georgetown and Columbia Universities.

He has written a large number of books and articles on Palestinian and Arab political history, including *Under Siege: PLO Decisionmaking during the 1982 War* (1986) and *British Policy towards Syria and Palestine, 1906–1914* (1980).

JUDITH KIPPER
Guest Scholar, Brookings Institution
Ms. Kipper, a Middle East specialist, is a guest scholar at the Brookings Institution. As Senior Program Associate, she directs the Council on Foreign Relations Middle East Forum in Washington. She is a consultant on international affairs to the Rand Corporation and ABC News.

SAMUEL W. LEWIS
President, United States Institute of Peace
Ambassador Lewis's thirty-one years in the Foreign Service included tours with the National Security Council, as Deputy Director of the Policy Planning Staff, as Assistant Secretary of State for International Organization Affairs, and as Ambassador to Israel for eight years under Presidents Carter and Reagan. He participated in the Camp David meetings and all phases of Egypt-Israel and Lebanon-Israel negotiations between 1977 and 1985. Since retirement he has lectured and written extensively on Middle East issues.

IAN S. LUSTICK
Dartmouth College
Professor Lustick is an Associate Professor of Government at Dartmouth College specializing in Middle Eastern and international politics. He is the author of *Arabs in the Jewish State: Israel's Control of a National Minority* (1980) and *For the Land and the Lord: Jewish Fundamentalism in Israel* (forthcoming).

CHARLES MCC. MATHIAS
Jones, Day, Reavis & Pogue
Senator Mathias is currently a partner in the law firm of Jones, Day, Reavis & Pogue. He served as Senator from Maryland from 1969 to 1987. As a member of the Senate Foreign Relations Committee, Senator Mathias was actively involved with Middle East issues.

FOUAD MOUGHRABI

University of Tennessee at Chattanooga
Professor Moughrabi is Professor of Political Science at the University of Tennessee and Director of the International Center for Research and Public Policy. He is the author of *Public Opinion and the Palestine Question* (1987).

ROBERT NEUMANN

Center for Strategic and International Studies
Ambassador Neumann is Senior Adviser and Director of Middle East programs at CSIS, Chairman of the American-Saudi Roundtable, and Chairman of the executive committee of the Moroccan-American Foundation. He was Ambassador to Afghanistan from 1966 to 1973; to Morocco from 1973 to 1976; and to Saudi Arabia in 1981. He was Director of the Department of State Transition Team for the Reagan administration in 1980–81.

WILLIAM B. QUANDT

Senior Fellow, Brookings Institution
Mr. Quandt was a member of the National Security Council staff from 1972 to 1974 and from 1977 to 1979. During the latter period, he participated in the negotiations that resulted in the Camp David Accords and the Egyptian-Israeli peace treaty. Since 1979 he has been a Senior Fellow at the Brookings Institution. During 1987–88, he served as President of the Middle East Studies Association. His most recent publication is *Camp David: Peacemaking and Politics* (1986).

HAROLD H. SAUNDERS

Visiting Fellow, Brookings Institution
Dr. Saunders served on the National Security Council staff from 1961 to 1974, and in the State Department from 1974 to 1981. He was Assistant Secretary of State for Near Eastern and South Asian Affairs from 1978 to 1981. He participated in the disengagement negotiations in 1973–75, and helped draft the Camp David Accords and the Egyptian-Israeli peace treaty. He wrote *The Other Walls: The Politics of the Arab-Israeli Peace Process* (1986).

HENRY SIEGMAN

American Jewish Congress
Mr. Siegman is the Executive Director of the American Jewish Congress. He was formerly Executive Secretary of the American

Association for Middle East Studies and editor of its quarterly, *Middle East Studies*. He is well-traveled in the Middle East and met last January with the heads of state of Egypt, Jordan, and Israel.

KENNETH WOLLACK
National Democratic Institute for International Affairs
Mr. Wollack is the Executive Vice President of the National Democratic Institute for International Affairs. He was formerly coeditor of the Middle East Policy Survey (1980–86) and legislative director of the American Israel Public Affairs Committee (1973–86).

CASIMIR A. YOST
Executive Director, World Affairs Council of Northern California
As foreign policy adviser to Senator Charles McC. Mathias (1977–1982), and while on the professional staff of the Senate Committee on Foreign Relations (1982–86), Mr. Yost devoted considerable attention to Middle East issues.